Titanic

THE DISASTER THAT SHOCKED THE WORLD!

By Mark Dubowski

Series Editor Deborah Lock
Art Editor C. David Gillingwater, Tanvi Nathyal
Senior Art Editor Clare Shedden
U.S. Editor Regina Kahney, Shannon Beatty
Pre-production producer Francesca Wardell
Picture Researcher Marie Osborn, Aditya Chopra
Jacket Designer Natalie Godwin, Martin Wilson
DTP Designer Anita Yadav
Managing Editor Soma B. Chowdhury
Managing Art Editor Ahlawat Gunjan
Indexer Lynn Bresler

Reading Consultant
Linda Gambrell, Ph.D.

First American Edition, 1998
Other editions, 2012
This edition, 2015
Published in the United States by DK Publishing
345 Hudson Street, New York, New York 10014

15 16 17 18 19 10 9 8 7 6 5 4 3 2 1
001—270536—June/15

A catalog record for this book is available
from the Library of Congress.

ISBN: 978-1-4654-2840-0 (Paperback)
ISBN: 978-1-4654-3018-2 (Hardcover)

DK books are available at special discounts when purchased in bulk for sales promotions,
premiums, fund-raising, or educational use. For details, contact:
DK Publishing Special Markets
345 Hudson Street, New York, New York 10014
SpecialSales@dk.com

Printed and bound in China

The publisher would like to thank the following for their kind permission to reproduce their photographs:
(Key: a=above, b=below/bottom, c=center, l=left, r=right, t=top)
Bridgeman Art Library, London / New York: Giraudon 32cr.
Corbis UK Ltd: Front jacket, 2tr, 2br, 20br, 30tc, 31.
Ecoscene: 22cb; Peter Hillme 24. **Mary Evans Picture Library:** 32tl.
Robert Harding Picture Library: 3, 15, 16tr, 16-17; Vulcan 15.
N.H.P.A.: Brian Hawks 27. **Oxford Scientific Films:** Anne Head 14.
Pa Photos: 4. **Planet Earth Pictures:** 13, 19c, 23tc; Dorian Wiesel 29.
Science Photo Library: 5; David Halpern 25; NASA 32br;
Peter Ryan 26. **Frank Spooner Pictures:** 9. **Tony Stone Images:**
Back jacket, 7. **Topham Picturepoint:** 12tc, 18bc, 32cl.
Jacket images: Front: **Corbis:** National Geographic Society / Raymond Wong.
Back: **Corbis:** Underwood & Underwood (tl).
All other images © Dorling Kindersley
For further information see: www.dkimages.com

A WORLD OF IDEAS:
SEE ALL THERE IS TO KNOW

www.dk.com

Contents

The Greatest Ship

When the White Star Line announced the completion of the "supership"—the *Titanic*—in 1912, they said that she was the greatest ship ever built: luxurious, unsinkable, and unbelievably big.

How big was she? The *Titanic* was more than 882 feet (269 meters) long. That's the length of 22 buses lined up end to end. She was the largest movable object in the world. When the *Titanic* passed a small ship, she was like a cloud going by. A big, black cloud that blotted out the sun.

The *Titanic*'s hull, or lower body, was divided into sixteen compartments. Up to four could flood and she would still be able to float.

The *Titanic* was like a floating palace. There were elegant restaurants, Turkish baths, and a swimming pool. Each class had separate rooms, lounges, and eating areas.

Reading and writing room

Gymnasium

First-class lounge

Private promenade

Third-class dining room

Sauna and steam room

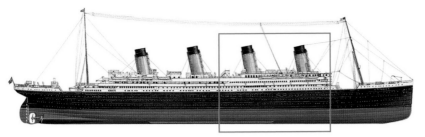

The section of the Titanic illustrated below is shown in this box.

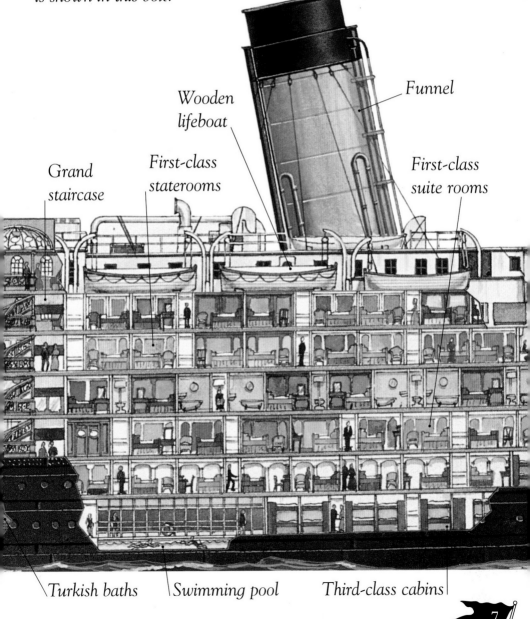

Wooden lifeboat

Funnel

First-class staterooms

Grand staircase

First-class suite rooms

Turkish baths

Swimming pool

Third-class cabins

7

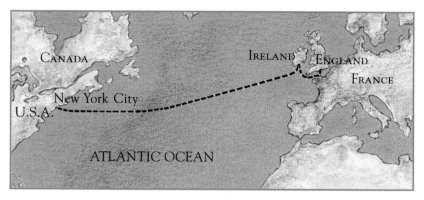

On her route, the Titanic *would also dock in France and Ireland to pick up passengers.*

On her maiden or first voyage she would sail across the Atlantic, from England to New York City.

In charge of the *Titanic* was Captain

Edward J. Smith. He would navigate from the bridge at the front of the ship. This was to be his last voyage before retiring.

Captain Edward J. Smith

Newspapers called the ship "the Millionaires' Special," but its passengers were really from all walks of life.

John Jacob Astor and his wife had first-class tickets. They were among the wealthiest passengers and had a suite, or group of rooms, fit for a king.

Colonel John Jacob Astor and his wife, Madeleine.

Not-so-rich people were going, too. Many were emigrants—with all their possessions in their luggage—hoping to start a new life in America.

All Aboard!

At last the *Titanic* is ready to set sail from England, teeming with more than a thousand passengers. Among them are dozens of children. Edmond and Michel Navratil from France are traveling in second class with their father. They are only two and three years old.

Crowds on the dock are waving flags and handkerchiefs. Some are cheering, while others are shouting, "Good luck, *Titanic*!" Passengers wave good-bye to friends and family.

The Astors' dog, named Kitty, came with them and was kept in kennels and exercised every day.

RMS TITANIC

Introducing the Largest and Finest Steamer in the World

Maiden Voyage
Sail from Southampton, England
to New York City, US

April 10–April 17, 1912

Revolutionary design,
Extraordinary dimensions
New 46,000 Tons
2,648 Passengers 899 Crew

Accommodation

Excellent value (price per person shown)

First Class

Lavish and spacious private staterooms include sitting room, two bedrooms, and two dressing rooms. Equipped with telephones, heaters, electrical fans, and steward call bells.

Multi-room parlor suites $2,500

Also available: Kennels for pets and single-berth cabins for servants $150

Second Class

Well-furnished staterooms include sink with mirror, and bed linen changed every day.
One-berth or two-berth staterooms $60

Third Class *(up to 6 people per cabin)*

Clean cabins with bunks include wardrobe space, sink with mirror, and lighting. Bed linen provided.
Two-berth stateroom $40

Danger Ahead!

 April 13

After three days at sea, the trip has seemed like a vacation for most of the passengers. But soon the *Titanic* will be entering an area of the north Atlantic Ocean where icebergs float.

April 14 11:40 P.M. All day the *Titanic* had received iceberg warnings in Morse code over the wireless telegraph. Now, as the ship speeds through the night, lookouts watch for icebergs from the crow's nest.

All is quiet on this freezing-cold night, and the ocean is incredibly calm. But then, with their watch about to come to an end, the lookouts see a dark object looming ahead. It is an iceberg . . . and the *Titanic* is heading straight toward it!

Quickly one of the lookouts sounds
the alarm bell and shouts into the
telephone connected to the bridge,
"Iceberg right ahead!"

With no time to waste, the First Officer calls for the ship's wheel to be turned as far as possible. Then he orders the engines to be stopped and put into reverse.

High in the crow's nest, the lookouts brace themselves for a collision as the iceberg looms closer and closer. Slowly, the ship starts to veer away from the iceberg. But, too late! There is a slight bump and a ripping noise as the iceberg scrapes the starboard side of the *Titanic*.

Many passengers are asleep. The small bump to the ship isn't enough to disturb them. But it wakes up Captain Smith. He rushes to the bridge to find out what happened.

Down below, the men working in one of the boiler rooms are almost swept off their feet as water gushes into the room. Within minutes the water is waist-high.

Automatic doors begin to seal the flooding compartments. The men rush to escape before they shut. But the water is rising higher and higher and flowing over the tops of the compartments, flooding one after another.

April 15 12:05 A.M. "Uncover the boats," Captain Smith orders his crew. Then he instructs the two wireless operators to start signaling for help. He knows the *Titanic* is going to sink— and he knows that there are not enough lifeboats to get all the passengers off safely.

Not far from the panic in the boiler rooms, many passengers are still fast asleep, unaware of the collision.

Out on the third-class deck, a few passengers find chunks of ice and start playing soccer. They have no idea how much danger they are in.

April 15 12:30 A.M. It is now past midnight. Many passengers come up from their rooms in their pajamas, but some are still wearing their evening clothes.

Colonel Astor and his wife make their way to the gymnasium next to the boat deck. While they wait for the crew to get a lifeboat ready, Colonel Astor cuts through a spare life jacket to show his wife what is inside.

Now the crew begins to direct the passengers into the boats. "Women and children first!" they shout.

Lifeboats are slowly lowered into the ocean by ropes,
which pass through the pulleys on cranes, called davits.

The crew lowers the first lifeboat 60 feet (18 meters) down to the ocean. But there are only 28 people in a boat for 65. The passengers don't want to leave the *Titanic*. The lifeboats seem unsteady compared to the big ship. The band is even playing cheerful music.

One by one the lifeboats are lowered, when disaster looms. Boat number 13 drifts under another lifeboat that is being lowered. The boat nearly crashes on top of number 13. At the last moment, a passenger frees the ropes holding number 13 and the boat floats away to safety.

As the lifeboats are lowered, lights are seen on the horizon—another ship is out there! It is far away, but the crew of the *Titanic* has a way to get its attention. They fire distress rockets that explode like fireworks in the sky. Then they use the Morse lamp. But there is no response.

Titanic's wireless operators keep calling for help. Although other ships are close enough, the wireless operators on some of these ships are asleep.

The *Olympic*, the *Titanic*'s sister ship, has heard the distress call. But she is too far away to be able to help.

Emergency Information

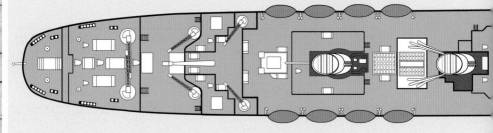

If an Emergency Evacuation is ordered, make your way to the top deck.

IMPORTANT

☞ Put on a life jacket.
☞ Listen to instructions from the crew.
☞ They will direct you to a lifeboat.
☞ Women and children to evacuate first.

There is room for an additional 16 lifeboats but this would clutter the decks and restrict your comfort during the journey.

Information key

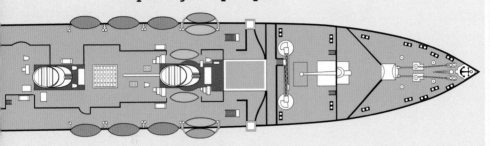

- 14 lifeboats: capacity 65 people
- 2 lifeboats: capacity 40 people
- 4 collapsible lifeboats: capacity 47 people

Life jackets

Life jackets are stowed in your cabin.
There is one for each person aboard.

 Put your life jacket on over your head.

 Bring the lower side straps around to the front.

 Tie the straps together securely across your chest.

 Do the same to the upper side straps.

Material: cork floats covered with canvas

The Final Hour

April 15 1:15 A.M. Slowly, slowly, the bow sinks farther. Slowly, slowly, the stern rises above it.

The band plays on, trying to keep the passengers calm. But everyone realizes now that the *Titanic* cannot be saved.

April 15 2:05 A.M. The last wooden lifeboat is about to be lowered.

Colonel Astor is waving good-bye to his wife. He is not allowed to board.

With more than 1,500 passengers still left, the crew has formed a protective circle around the lifeboat so that only women and children can take the last few seats.

Colonel Astor rushes to the kennels, where his dog Kitty is kept. He sets all the dogs free so they will not be trapped.

Michel and Edmond Navratil are still on the ship. Their father has wrapped them in blankets to keep them warm. Their only hope of escape is in the last collapsible boat about to be launched. Their father pushes forward and hands them to a woman sitting in the boat. Then he steps back into the crowd.

April 15 2:17 A.M. The music has stopped now, but the ship's lights are still glowing in the dark. As the stern rises higher into the air, everything inside the ship slides to the bow. Pianos, furniture, statues, paintings, dishes, luggage—every object on board crashes down and piles up.

Out on the deck there are still hundreds of passengers. The slant on the deck is so steep now that they cannot stand up straight. Some are clinging desperately to the rails. Others lose their grip and fall into the sea. It is a long drop, like a fall from a tall building.

Those wearing life jackets are kept afloat. But the water is ice-cold and they will soon freeze to death if they are not rescued.

The *Titanic*'s lights flicker as she plunges . . . then she's gone. People in the water scream for help, but their cries soon die down. The survivors huddle together, cold and afraid.

Here in the north Atlantic, there is no first, second, or third class. Rich and poor, young and old—they are all in this together now. All of them hoping to survive, none of them knowing what will happen next.

The survivors in the lifeboats had rowed away from the ship. They feared that they would either be sucked down with the *Titanic* as she sank or be swamped by the people in the water.

But now some sailors decide to row back to the floating wreckage of the *Titanic*.

They want to see if anyone is still alive. They row through hundreds of frozen bodies and find just four survivors. One dies shortly afterward.

Lost and Saved

This bar chart shows the numbers
of people lost and saved among
the three classes and crew.

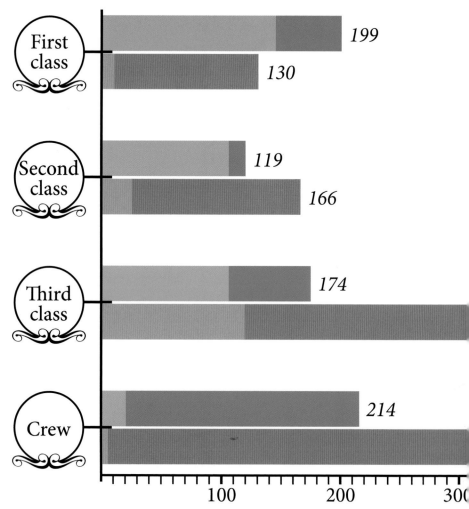

First class — 199
First class — 130

Second class — 119
Second class — 166

Third class — 174

Crew — 214

100 200 300

Numbers of people (based on the findings of the

Conclusion

The numbers of those who survived varied greatly among the three classes and crew. Since there was no passenger list, the real number of people who lost their lives will never be known.

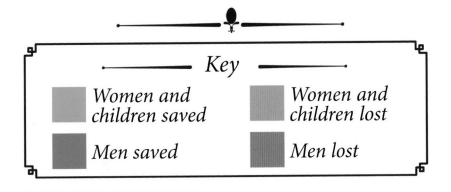

Key

- Women and children saved
- Women and children lost
- Men saved
- Men lost

536

685

| 400 | 500 | 600 | 700 |

American inquiry about the sinking of the *Titanic*)

The Rescue

It is almost dawn. The survivors have been at sea for several hours now, without food, water, or warm clothing. Many are almost frozen to death. Suddenly, they see rockets in the distance. Another ship is on its way—help has arrived!

It is the *Carpathia*. Her crew had heard the *Titanic's* distress calls. But the ship was 58 miles (93 kilometers) away—a three-hour trip. She has arrived too late to save the people in the water, but not too late to save the people in the lifeboats.

The Carpathia *had raced through the dangerous ice fields after receiving the distress message.*

One by one, the *Titanic* survivors board the *Carpathia*. Some climb a rope ladder to reach the deck of the ship. Others who are too weak or too young to climb are hauled aboard in cargo nets. Everyone is counted: of the 2,206 passengers, only 705 people have survived.

The *Carpathia* now heads for New York. The journey will take three days.

The dazed survivors are given warm clothes and food.

April 18 Friends and relatives have been frantic for news. They are confused by the different reports. The *Carpathia* is not releasing any information, and newspapers are making up stories. One says everyone survived and that the *Titanic* is being towed by another ship. Other newspapers say many have died.

In New York, people wait anxiously for the *Carpathia*, hoping they will see their loved ones step off the ship.

People start to wait along the pier in New York.

Newspapers are filled with conflicting stories of the disaster.

April 18 **9:25 P.M.** At last the *Carpathia* sails into New York harbor. Nearly 30,000 people are lining the dock. Among them are many doctors and nurses sent to help the survivors.

The gangplank is lowered from the *Carpathia* and the first survivors walk down. People on the dock rush forward. Some call out the names of their relatives.

Harold Bride, the only surviving wireless operator, is carried off the ship. His feet are badly frostbitten and have been bandaged. Also among the survivors are two dogs.

The grateful survivors of the Titanic *disaster presented this medal to the crew of the* Carpathia *for saving their lives.*

Harold Bride was washed overboard as the Titanic sank.
He managed to climb on to an overturned lifeboat.

Michel and Edmond Navratil with their mother

Michel and Edmond Navratil are safe. They are being looked after by a survivor until they can be reunited with their mother, Marcelle, in France. She did not know that they were on the *Titanic*.

The children's father had been separated from their mother and had kidnapped the boys. He had told travelers that their mother was dead. Marcelle recognized her sons from a photograph in a French newspaper, telling the tragic story about the two "orphaned" boys.

Mrs. Astor is among the survivors. She had helped to row her lifeboat away from the sinking *Titanic*.

Out in the ocean, ships are finding bodies of the victims. Many of them cannot be identified. But Colonel Astor's body is identified. His initials were printed on his shirt collar.

Captain Smith's body is not found among the 328 bodies recovered. Some reports say that he was standing on the bridge before the ship sank.

Heroes and Heroines

Whether rich or poor, every survivor had a remarkable tale to tell. There were also some remarkable acts of bravery.

Molly Brown
1st-class passenger
Lifeboat number 6
She took command of the lifeboat and encouraged the other women on board the lifeboat to also row with great determination toward the rescue ship.

Countess of Rothes
1st-class passenger
Lifeboat number 8
In the lifeboat, she took her turn at the oars as well as at the tiller for most of the night.

Fifth Officer Lowe
Crew
Lifeboat number 14
He commanded his lifeboat to go back and look for survivors, pulling four people from the water.

The *Titanic* musicians
Crew
Went down with the ship
After the collision, they played a selection of songs to keep the passengers' spirits lifted until the very end.

Women in the lifeboats helped to hand out blankets and comforted each other. Others gave up their personal letters to be burned as signals. Many put the safety of others before their own.

Discovered

In the years after the *Titanic* sank, many people wanted to find her. But the ship's exact location was a mystery, and the technology didn't exist to reach her even if her whereabouts had been known. The *Titanic* had plunged 12,460 feet (3,798 meters)—that's the height of ten Empire State buildings!

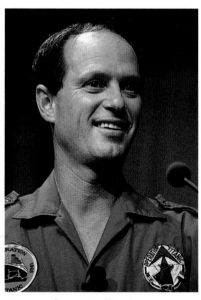

Dr. Robert Ballard was the scientist in charge of the expedition.

More than 70 years passed. Then in 1985 a team led by Dr. Robert Ballard used an unmanned diving vessel called *Argo*. *Argo* had a video camera that sent pictures back to the research ship.

The explorers sent *Argo* down to the bottom of the ocean. Day after day *Argo* searched the seabed for signs of the wreck but saw nothing.

Then one day an object appeared on the monitor of the research ship—it was an image of a huge boiler. The *Titanic* had been found! She had broken into two and her contents spilled across the seabed.

This is an image of the front of a boiler, which was found lying on the Atlantic seabed.

The Titanic had 29 boilers. The picture above shows the boilers before they were installed on the Titanic.

The Nautile, *a small submersible, was carried by a special research ship to the site of the wreck and then launched.*

Two years later, another submersible, the *Nautile* (naw-TEEL), visited the *Titanic*. It was equipped with the latest technology, including a movable video camera that could film inside the rooms of the *Titanic*.

The *Nautile* also had two robotic arms, which were operated by a pilot inside the submersible. These arms had different attachments that enabled the pilot to pick up various types of objects.

The *Nautile* brought back thousands of ordinary objects that were scattered over the seabed: toys, eyeglasses, money, and jewels. They were all that remained of the *Titanic*'s victims.

Once on dry land, the objects were carefully cleaned and restored so that they could be displayed in exhibitions. These objects helped tell the story of the *Titanic* and her passengers.

Nautile's robotic arm is used to pick up this safe. Part of the safe had rotted away, and it was empty.

This money was also retrieved by the Nautile. *It was found inside a bag that was lying on the seabed.*

Nautile's technology also enabled scientists to answer a question that had remained a mystery since the sinking: What really did happen to the *Titanic*?

Nautile's evidence showed that the iceberg did not carve a 300-foot (91-meter) gash along the side of the *Titanic* as suspected. Instead, the iceberg had made six small cuts below the waterline, which had allowed the water to gush into her hull.

By examining the wreck of the *Titanic*, scientists were also able to explain exactly how she broke apart.

How the *Titanic* sank

1. The *Titanic* hits the iceberg, which scrapes the ship in six places. Water gushes in through the narrow openings.

2. The compartments flood, one after another. The weight of the water in the bow starts to pull the ship under.

3. The front funnel collapses. Then, as the stern rises into the air, the other funnels also start to crash under the strain.

4. The strain on the ship is so great that she breaks apart. The bow plunges to the bottom. The stern starts to flood and then sinks.

Tour of the Ocean Floor

Welcome inside the *Nautile*. For the next six hours, we will take a tour around the site of the *Titanic's* wreck. It will take us about 90 minutes to descend 12,470 ft (3,800 m) to the site. The debris field is a square about 1 mile (2.6 km) across and along. You will need to lie down flat and look through your porthole. The spotlights of the *Nautile* will light up the various parts.

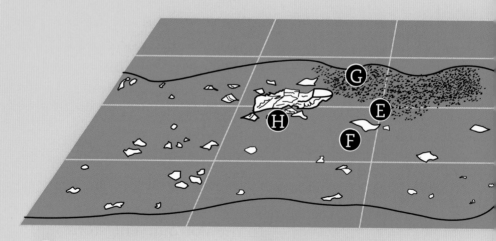

A *The bridge*

B *The bow and crow's nest*

C *The public areas*

D *The debris field*

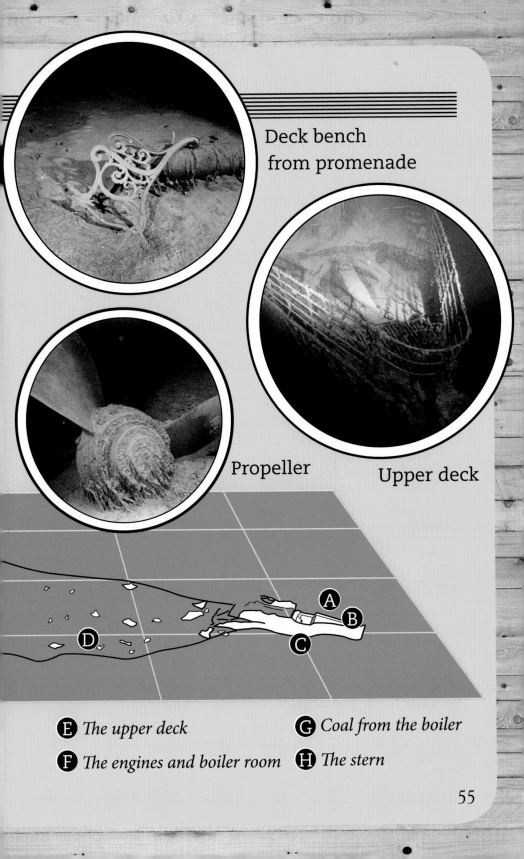

Deck bench
from promenade

Propeller

Upper deck

E *The upper deck*

F *The engines and boiler room*

G *Coal from the boiler*

H *The stern*

55

Lessons of the *Titanic*

When the *Titanic* sank in 1912 a full inquiry was launched at the time. Many questions were asked: Would the *Titanic* have sunk if she had not sailed at full speed on that fatal night? Was her design at fault?

All these issues were discussed. But more importantly, new safety regulations for passenger liners were passed.

Ships had to carry enough lifeboats for everyone. Wireless operators had to listen to their radios all night long. A special airborne Ice Patrol was set up to help warn ships of dangerous icebergs.

Never again would people dare call any ship "unsinkable." The *Titanic* was a cruel lesson for everyone.

Michel Navratil talks to another survivor at a Titanic reunion in 1996. He could recall being placed in a sack and then hauled to safety on board the Carpathia.

Iceberg Up Close

What are icebergs?

Icebergs are huge chunks of ice that have broken away from ice sheets and glaciers. Ocean tides, currents, and waves break up these chunks of ice. Some chunks are so large that they last for many years before melting in warmer waters.

Why is only 10% of an iceberg visible?

When water freezes it expands. The ice uses the same amount of water but takes up more space. This means that the density of the ice is slightly less than that of the water around it, so it floats. But this amount is only a 10% difference, so the rest of the ice is below the water.

Titanic Quiz

1. What was the route of the *Titanic's* maiden voyage?

2. At what time did the *Titanic* hit the iceberg?

3. How many people were in the first lifeboat?

4. What was the name of the ship that came to the rescue?

5. How had the iceberg damaged the *Titanic*?

Answers on page 61.

Glossary

Boiler
A furnace that boils water to create steam. This powers the ship.

Bow
The front part of a ship.

Bridge
An area at the front of a ship from which it is steered.

Collapsible boat
A boat with canvas sides, which can be collapsed so that the boat can be stored easily.

Crow's nest
A platform on a ship's mast from which lookouts watch for danger.

Davits
Crane-like mechanisms used for holding or lowering lifeboats.

Dock
A place where ships arrive and depart.

Emigrants
People who move from one country to live in another.

First class
The highest level of comfort on a ship. People who go first class pay a higher fare than others.

Funnel
A pipe or chimney that enables smoke from the boiler room to escape.

Hull
A ship's body.

Lifeboat
A boat used by people if they have to abandon ship.

Maiden voyage
The first time a ship makes a journey in service.

Morse code
A system of dots and dashes for each letter of the alphabet.

Morse lamp
A lamp used to flash distress signals in Morse code.

Propellers
Shafts with blades. A ship's engines drive the propellers around and this pushes a ship forward.

Rocket
A small device that makes a bright light in the sky. Used as a distress signal.

Second class
A level of comfort that is not as expensive as first class and with fewer services.

Starboard
The right-hand side of a ship when facing the front of a ship.

Stern
The rear part of a ship.

Submersible
A boat that travels underwater.

Third class
The lowest level of comfort on a ship. People in third class pay the lowest fare and get very few services.

Wireless
A telegraph machine that sends messages by radio waves.

Index

Answers to the *Titanic* Quiz:

1. England to New York City, US, via France and Ireland;
2. 11:40 P.M.; **3.** 28; **4.** *Carpathia*; **5.** Made six small cuts in hull.

Guide for Parents

DK Readers is a four-level interactive reading adventure series for children, developing the habit of reading widely for both pleasure and information. These books have an exciting main narrative interspersed with a range of reading genres to suit your child's reading ability, as required by the Common Core State Standards. Each book is designed to develop your child's reading skills, fluency, grammar awareness, and comprehension in order to build confidence and engagement when reading.

Ready for a *Reading Alone* book

YOUR CHILD SHOULD

- be able to read most words without needing to stop and break them down into sound parts.

- read smoothly, in phrases and with expression. By this level, your child will be mostly reading silently.

- self-correct when some word or sentence doesn't sound right.

A VALUABLE AND SHARED READING EXPERIENCE

For some children, text reading, particularly non-fiction, requires much effort, but adult participation can make this both fun and easier. So here are a few tips on how to use this book with your child.

TIP 1 Check out the contents together before your child begins:

- invite your child to check the blurb, contents page, and layout of the book and comment on it.

- ask your child to make predictions about the story.

- talk about the information your child might want to find out.

TIP 2 Encourage fluent and flexible reading:

- support your child to read in fluent, expressive phrases, making full use of punctuation and thinking about the meaning.

- encourage your child to slow down and check information where appropriate.

TIP 3 Indicators that your child is reading for meaning:

- your child will be responding to the text if he/she is self-correcting and varying his/her voice.
- your child will want to talk about what he/she is reading or is eager to turn the page to find out what will happen next.

TIP 4 Share and discuss:

- encourage your child to recall specific details after each chapter.
- provide opportunities for your child to pick out interesting words and discuss what they mean.
- discuss how the author captures the reader's interest, or how effective the non-fiction layouts are.
- ask questions about the text. These help to develop comprehension skills and awareness of the language used.

A FEW ADDITIONAL TIPS

- Read to your child regularly to demonstrate fluency, phrasing, and expression; to find out or check information; and for sharing enjoyment.
- Encourage your child to reread favorite texts to increase reading confidence and fluency.
- Check that your child is reading a range of different types of material, such as poems, jokes, and following instructions.

Series consultant, **Dr. Linda Gambrell**, Distinguished Professor of Education at Clemson University, has served as President of the National Reading Conference, the College Reading Association, and the International Reading Association. She is also reading consultant for the **DK Adventures**.

Have you read these other great books from DK?

READING ALONE

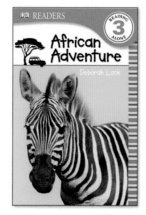

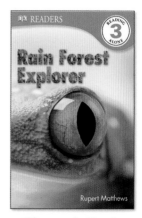

Meet the sharks who live on the reef or come passing through.

Experience the thrill of seeing wild animals on an African safari.

Through Zoe's blog, discover the mysteries of the Amazon.

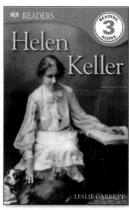

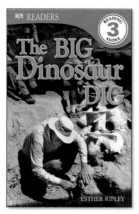

Read about the remarkable story of the deaf-blind girl who achieved great things.

Josh and his team dig up dinosaur bones in a race against time.

Find out about the lives of six creepy spiders from around the world.